Time Travel

poems by

Suzanne M. Carey

Finishing Line Press
Georgetown, Kentucky

Time Travel

ACKNOWLEDGMENTS

"Blue Ridge Detour"—an earlier version was published as "Lost and Found"—
Mountain High, A Poetry Anthology, 2008
"Rituals"—*New Ohio Review* 12, Fall 2012
"Memorial"—*Cradle Songs, An Anthology of Poems on Motherhood,* May 2012
"Carolina Sunset"—*The Women's Review of Books,* January/February 2013
"Late Summer Evening"—*The Women's Review of Books,* January/February 2013
"The Model"—*Kansas City Voices,* Volume 11, Whispering Prairie Press, 2013
"In the Gallery"—*Kansas City Voices,* Volume 11, Whispering Prairie Press, 2013
"Summer Night"—*New Ohio Review* 17, Spring 2015

Editor: Christen Kincaid

Cover Art: Suzanne M. Carey

Author Photo: Michael J. Carey

Cover Design: Elizabeth Maines

Printed in the USA on acid-free paper.
Order online: www.finishinglinepress.com
          also available on amazon.com

Author inquiries and mail orders:
Finishing Line Press
P. O. Box 1626
Georgetown, Kentucky 40324
U. S. A.

Table of Contents

Late Summer Evening...1

Tomatoes..2

Rituals 3

Memorial 4

Reflection on the Window 5

Nativity..6

Winter Afternoon...7

Grief 8

The Dormitory...9

April 1968 10

Time Travel...11

Italy, 1967, 2014 12

Coffee 13

Blue Ridge Detour 14

Carolina Sunset...15

Turtle..16

The Painter 17

Nude...18

The Model...19

In the Gallery 20

Wormhole...22

Bones..23

Summer Night...24

On the Back Deck, Late August..25

Gone 26

For Michael, Cristin, and Patrick Carey
with love and appreciation

Late Summer Evening

My brother is dead.
So are my mother and father.
But I am here
in my study,

drinking Jack Daniels,
listening to the washer
spin my swim towel,
my husband's shorts,

watching the breeze riffle
the fading blue morning glories
atop my neighbor's roof.
As colors soften,

more ghosts creep in:
my sister-in-law, who shrank
from life's ledges, spirals from
the Holiday Inn's twelfth floor;

my surfer boyfriend loses his grip
a few rungs from the rescue copter's
hatch and plummets back into the sea,
death so often coming from Icarian heights.

I swirl my sweating glass,
crazed cubes clacking
like dice in a leather cup.

Tomatoes

Summer arrived late in August, finally
hot enough to ripen the tomatoes,
plump beefsteaks cascading from vines,
careening, wild and wobbly,
bold and succulent, through the garden.

When my mother was a girl,
she sprinkled salt on sun-warmed tomatoes
and ate them like apples,
juice dripping through her fingers
onto her blouse and bare feet,

her days abundant before she grew,
married, and moved to a suburban house
where all that flourished was a giant chestnut
with spiny pods and immense shade
that stunted the tomatoes.

Rituals

After my swim, I sit at a small table at Peet's
with my medium sugar-free, low fat, vanilla freddo
that the barista started as I walked in.
I push the whipped cream deep into the glass and worry

about my daughter, who drives
a perilously small car on the freeway,
and my son in New Orleans, too poor to drive,
whose illness frightens me most of all.

My father worried about us until the day he died.
When I came home from college, he insisted
I take the dog or my ten-year old brother with me
when I drove at night. At 86, he called me daily

from the nursing home to make sure I was okay.
I remember how my mother savored
half a nickel box of licorice bits and a single cigarette
as she read each evening, waiting for us to come home,

and years later, how she devoured the Hershey bars
and Cokes Dad brought her every afternoon,
long after she had forgotten us all.

Memorial

I take my mother from the trunk
of the car, surprisingly heavy
in a plush crimson bag with gold cord,
cloaked like fine scotch.

I don't want to feel the shape of her box,
refuse to prod her ashes. She never found me
thin or blonde or pretty enough;
she loved a beautiful package.

Fourteen hours after she, finally, died,
my brother and I, exhausted, in grubby jeans,
savored fillet and chocolate cake, toasted her
with cabernet at the Monkey Cat,

all possibility of pleasing
her, at last, gone.

Reflection on the Window

As I stride past the children's shop's riot
of knits, plaids, smocking and appliqué,
the crayon-bright slickers and rain boots stop me.
I want to buy a pair of tiny green rubbers
with bulgy black frog eyes and a smile at the toes,
a shiny red raincoat with snaps, perhaps
a blue sweater flung with kites or balloons.
I want to take them home, tuck them into a bed-
room bureau, as I did so many years ago,
eagerly awaiting puddle-splash days
and sweaters shrugged off in a sandbox.

Nativity

Every year, I look out the window
and admire our neighbor's Christmas tree
with golden lights beaming,
up two weeks before I reluctantly buy ours.

There must have been a time when I loved Christmas, too.
I have boxes of icicle lights, a hand-painted angel,
snowman stockings and red and green porch banners
I sewed when our children were small.

I doubt Mary suspected what lay ahead when she first
held her son. Years after the magi departed and the star set,
did she long for the stink of the cattle, the milk in her breast,
the cold isolation of those nights when she believed
she could, perhaps, protect him?

Winter Afternoon

I set ingredients
on the counter in neat clusters,
one each for cake and soup.
Pot, pans, bowls, spoons
gleam in desolation.
The unset table
longs for cloth and silver,
ritual grace, food and chatter
to fill the cracks,
to glaze the day
like sun on snow.

Grief

I have burned to my edges so many times
I am wisps of soot in passion's wake.

I am the bride on the dock, battleship steaming out,
the mother as her child is wheeled into emergency.

In the locker room, dripping from the shower,
I lean onto a friend's shoulder as she sobs, too,

one grief rekindling another, unquenchable.

The Dormitory

I often dream I am back at college,
in a stairwell, climbing concrete steps,
pulling open fire doors,
entering linoleum corridors
to see if my room is there.

The rooms have faded yellow walls.
Tight trapezoids of sunlight bleach
the naked floors. The bookshelves
are empty, the mattresses bare,
the roommates never present,
though sometimes I glimpse
a shadow in the hall.

I look at my hands,
the skin wrinkled seersucker,
my wedding band embedded in flesh,
and flee, searching for my next class,
though I know I'll never find the room,
the place where I can start over.

April 1968

I remember our break up
on a jasmine-scented evening
sitting on the front steps
of the college row house where I lived
Softly, as I Leave You drifting through
the window of a first floor bedroom.
I cried and clung and for days
after lived on toast and tears.

Last I heard, he was working in an auto parts store,
living across the bay in the brown shingle-sided house
he once shared with his mother, a well-worn house
where I came to love Mozart, Bach, and Bruckner,
the house where we spent a year of weekends,
me starting the nights in his sister's childhood room.

He turns 72 this month, no doubt gray, wrinkles
crazing his tan face, eyes still as dark as the coffee
we drank with almond fudge sundaes.
I wonder if I'd recognize him. I want to drive
50 miles to find the ice cream shop, the house.

I want to regain the heat
of summer sidewalk under papery sandals,
the dusty scent of sycamores,
the thrill of an aria on the kitchen radio,
his mother's scaloppini
overflowing with wild mushrooms,
her yellow platter of green beans.

I want him to admire my beauty as I tell him
of my kids, my career, my happiness.
I want him to want me as I kiss him softly
and then go home.

Time Travel

How fast the foreign becomes the familiar.
How quickly old releases young.
Time and place bend and weave
until I have always awakened
to a rooster's crow and summer sun gliding
through gaps in wood-shuttered windows
recessed in stone walls half a millennium old
while breeze tousles the olive orchard,
and the toast-and-trout aroma of hillside
pastures pocked with grazing gray sheep
competes with the perfume of espresso.

Italian undulates around me.
Inexplicably, I respond with French
nouns and Spanish phrases.
I am as old as the rolling hills
and Etruscan ruins and as young as
my jeans flung over a rope
strung between two gnarled pines.
I watch them dance and dry in the wind,
my feet bare in the dying grass.

Italy, 1967, 2014

Blonde, thin, quintessentially American,
that monochrome winter in Rome
I refused to wear Europe's uniform—
black coat, shoes and purse.
I, instead, chose yellows and reds
and carelessly bloomed in snow
like a rogue rose or sprig of wild mustard
men in the streets attempted to pluck.
Italy was pizza, gelato, espresso,
cheap charms to chain to my bracelet,
grand paintings—dark and depressing—
and candles lit in cathedrals
where I went to beg for love.

Now, I blend into Umbrian hillsides
like a knob-kneed olive tree or nappy lamb
grazing by a gray stone wall, content
to let summer's ripening oranges
and bold begonias garner all attention.
I celebrate bruschetta, minestrone,
olive oil, *balsamico*, chunks of asiago,
heady Barolo, chilled prosecco,
kneel in chapels, pray to protect
the rich remains of family, friends,
and passion's lingering embers.

Coffee

I get together with a friend
I haven't seen in over a year.
Things are good—
her husband's cancer is in remission;
her daughter with the incurable genetic
disease has moved to Greece, owns a bar,
announced she's a lesbian, wants a baby;
her other daughter's ditched the addict
boyfriend and gone back to school.

We talk about when to begin
Social Security, who has died,
men we've loved. She mentions
a man we both once craved from afar
but neither of us ever pursued.
We recall his Alpine strength
and devilish wit before the stroke,
remember when we believed
life would keep getting better.

Blue Ridge Detour

The woman in Black Mountain told me
I could find glass beads in Morganton.
I stopped at a seafood inn
where the waitress couldn't tell me
if the salmon was wild or farm,
but she got me to the bead shop:
left, three lights, left, right.

The way back was less direct,
map misread, tight curves twisting
past Parkway gaps until a gravel road
slid me into a barn-like oasis where
I licked a melty Moose Tracks cone
perched in a white plastic chair,
listened to the Hit or Miss Band's

harmonica, banjo, fiddle, and three guitars,
and watched six gray couples in jeans
and shorts, plaid shirts and tees, dance
as if at their prom. A sixteen year old,
a good Christian boy, the leader said,
working this summer at the sawmill, sang,
and I wondered how hard it is to be

a Good Christian when you work
your muscles eight-times-five weekly,
sing with a band on Saturdays,
and on Sundays pray in the Baptist church
with a pretty Beckie you'll marry
after high school, and never leave
these bosky gaps and narrow roads.

Carolina Sunset

On the patio, we lean back in wooden rockers
as sun pinks beyond blue mountains,
a bottle of single malt between us on the flagstones.
We pass a plastic jar of cashews back and forth,
fingers brushing at each handoff, casually, as if
there'd never been a time when touching each other
was the most electric sensation in the universe,
as if we have always been as we are now,
graying, sipping whisky, talking of your dog,
my cat, our children, and our spouses.

Turtle

In elementary school, the nuns labeled you
disabled, slow, shrugged, tugged at their rosaries,
expected less from you, perhaps believing
your unrepentant left-handedness
and guarded grin justified their judgments.

When you watched an older brother draw a turtle
on a scrap of paper at the kitchen table, you learned
a pencil can translate a horned shell fortress
of flesh and breath into beauty, understood art,
not perfect cursive, was your way into the world.

The Painter

She took me to her apartment, showed me
the life-size portrait of her dead sister.
Sometimes cancer makes you thin,
sometimes it puffs you up, she said.
She'd painted a plump woman—blonde,
lively-eyed, melding, Matisse-like,
into a collage of Umbrian summer colors.

This sloe-eyed artist's body has shrunk.
Her pace is measured, her movements, spare,
as if we are given a unique allotment of passions,
journeys, and breaths, and once careless, she now
rations hers. I want to paint her portrait, want to
capture this state of entropy, the exquisite fading
before the painter exists only as the painted.

Nude

My boobs seem to dangle
from my neck like a string of buoys,
one eye is noticeably larger,
half my nose is missing, and
my strategically positioned glass
of red wine tips precariously,
but the instructor pronounces
my self-portrait *perfect*, says
the flaws are what make it *art*.
I thought I'd just fucked up again,
but he insists there is narrative
and captured spirit, and for a moment
I believe my mother's standards
of beauty and decorum were not infallible
and perfection doesn't matter.
But when I look again, I see my mouth
is crooked and long to make it right.

The Model

He is a handsome man—mid-forties, immaculate, well-hung—
unlike the worn, sagging characters we usually get.
It's not supposed to be like this: I know this man. I know
he is an attorney, a youth soccer coach, that his secretary
books these gigs, and I wonder if she has seen him naked,
if this is a kinky game they play. Unlike other models,

he undresses in front of us, which seems too intimate,
despite the fact we are in a bright, second floor studio
across from city hall, five women at easels, brushes poised.
It is difficult to separate man from model, to see him,
as our instructor says—grouped shapes, shades, line and form.
I think of male artists who both slept with their models and painted

the women they married. I try to imagine a man I adore, naked,
displayed in front of our class, all business, nothing personal.
I concentrate on gesture, how flesh segments space. I define shoulders,
sketch feet, shape jaw, capture the asymmetry of testicles drooping
in their pleated bag, how late afternoon light dapples skin. I paint
and paint until the man is lost in pigment and what emerges is the art.

In the Gallery

I am puzzling over the best-of-show painting
when an articulate apparition appears a few inches behind my left
    shoulder.
Without greeting or preface, he begins dissecting the work on the
    wall.
His manicured finger hovers over the canvas as he traces
layers of pigment and meaning, his gravel-edged voice confident.
Is he the man who kissed me wetly and a bit off-center last week
in my dream? I want him to do it again, right now, here

in front of this painting and its blue ribbon. I want him to slip his
    arm
around my waist and nudge me from this bright gallery to a dusky
    bistro,
where we will order a carafe of house red and meatball sandwiches,
and it will take a half-dozen napkins to wipe tomato sauce from
    between our fingers,
laughing, talking like I used to talk with men in the sixties, men
    who played guitar
and knew all of Dylan and Leonard Cohen and crooned *Suzanne*
in their candle-lit off-campus apartments before confessing they no
    longer loved me.

I *hmmmm* and nod as he speaks. I sense his height, catch the scent
    of citrus soap,
note his beveled wedding band. Is he young and earnest, trying to
    impress? Or older—
I his naïf to educate? If this were a movie or novel, by now our eyes
    would have met,
mine ribbon-blue, his God only knows what color (though I hope
    they are green),

but I don't dare look at him as he talks of tonality and texture. By
    now, we should,
at least, be strolling languidly toward the wine and cheese in the
    next room.
By now, if truth be told, I should be home feeding the cat, but
    instead I stay
in the gallery and stare at the painting, desperately in love with all
    of it.

Wormhole

The wonderful thing about being alive
is that you get to eat, everyday,
day after day, meal after meal,
coffee and granola with your newspaper,
cafe salads with friends or a sandwich
on a bench with a trashy magazine,
kitchen garlicky, dinner home-cooked,
wine in water glasses, then feet up,
drinking the remains of the bottle
before drifting off to dreams.

And you get to sleep, each night
a kaleidoscope recasting familiar
fantasies and fears. My perennial dream
of facing a final exam when I never
went to class refracts into an art opening
where I can't find you in the crowded gallery,
can't find anyone to help.

Perhaps tonight's twist will be better:
while scores natter and sip
sauvignon blanc in the lobby,
we will hold hands in front of some
god-awful abstract painting that sucks
us into its whirl of carmines and cadmiums,
then spins us into a shadowy space
where faceless waiters bring heaping platters
of linguini and carafes of red and white until
we drift through the walls, sated and unafraid.

Bones

My bones ache and wake me,
the left hip a steady pinch,
both legs below the knee feel
pounded by a ball peen hammer.

Later, espresso in hand, I sit
beside a lemon tree, watching
a green-backed lizard flick up
the stone wall and glide
into a tent of terra cotta,
no bones apparent in its body.

Generations lie in ossuaries,
skulls severed, body bones sorted,
femurs with femurs, ribs with ribs,
heart and brain now powdered spirit.

If bones resurrected
and randomly reassembled,
one shin shorter, one arm longer,
would my legs still ache
without my head?
Could my hand still scrawl a poem?

Summer Night

Teen boys shoot hoops
a few yards from my open door.
The night's nearly moonless,
yet they persist,
thunka-thunka of ball on blacktop
driving me to the verge of complaint,
like some old woman
in a numbing net of loneliness,
the old woman I suddenly am.

Today, the man I love told me
how he happened to leave Michigan
and mused how different
his life would have been if he'd stayed—
no degrees;
running a string of gas stations
or clocking in as a machinist like his dad;
never meeting his wife—

this last said with a shaky smile,
like someone who, by turning back
to retrieve a forgotten umbrella,
dodged death, and I realize finding her
is something he will never regret.
No matter how much he loves me
or how many cracks in his soul I caulk,
she is the rock he's built his life on.

Summer fades like worn denim,
yellowing leaves grow frail.
I close my door.
Outside the boys ceaselessly aim
at shadowy baskets
that cannot hold a thing.

On the Back Deck, Late August

At 3:20, piano practice begins
next door—deliberate and dutiful,
the youngest boy home from school.
By seven, the oldest will be on the bench,
his touch lighter, the music recognizable.

The UPS man rumbles into the cul de sac
earlier than usual with the weekly delivery
of kibble for the piano players' dog,
then thunks my latest books
onto our front porch.

It's been years since I've heard infants
cry as I sit reading in the sun,
most of the neighborhood children older
or like ours, grown and gone.
The only wails I hear now

are from a fire truck or ambulance
from the station up the street.
I hold my breath until I know
if they're racing toward us
or speeding away.

Gone

She did not believe in an afterlife,
yet when she learned she had only
a few weeks left, she asked me to put
pink roses on her daughter's grave
each year on her birthday.
Resigned to her own death,
she could not bear leaving
her only child alone and forgotten.

I often dream of my dead,
still think I will run into them downtown,
still start to call them when I hear news
of a mutual friend or a good joke or find
a place that makes cinnamon ice cream
like our freshman dorm served on Fridays.
In those moments, they shine before me.

Most of the time I am okay with absence,
but some days, I rail at doors now locked
and how time only flows in one direction
and can never be rewound.
Just when I think I've found a stable bluff,
I discover I am at the edge of a crumbling cliff,
clinging to clumps of wild grass,
craning my neck to peer over.

Born in San Francisco, **Suzanne Mackey Carey** earned B.A. and M.B.A. degrees from Stanford University, where she worked as a financial manager until retiring in 2009. She inadvertently refers to her retirement as her "graduation." It, indeed, marked the commencement of the happiest phase of her life so far. She fills her days with writing, printmaking, painting, swimming, and travel, activities she loves but could only squeeze into day's cracks during her finance career.

Suzanne studied writing for many pre-retirement years in the Stanford Continuing Studies Program and for eleven summers at the Wildacres Writers Workshop in North Carolina. Since retiring, she has participated in ongoing poetry workshops with Ellen Bass and Kim Addonizio.

Her work has been published in numerous journals and collections, including *New Ohio Review, Kansas City Voices, The Women's Review of Books, Red Wheelbarrow, Main Channel Voices,* and *Whetstone.* Her first chapbook, *George Washington Is Dead,* was also published by Finishing Line Press in 2012.

Suzanne has been married to Michael Carey for over forty-five years and has two grown children, Cristin and Patrick, of whom she extremely proud.